On the Sight of Angels

"From its early invitation to 'step into this / place where God is never / indifferent to the movement / of life' through its later invitation to 'look / for the corners visited by / radiant goodness,' *On the Sight of Angels* proves that Harold Recinos is alert to the messengers of God, and also 'unafraid to gather whatever / glitters in a world in need of / repair.'

—HL HIX,
Professor for the Department of Philosophy and the Creative Writing Program, University of Wyoming

"With incisive and prophetic prose, Harold Recinos uncovers the social maladies that meter alone cannot measure. His poetics accentuate lived life by evoking the undecidable syllables of pain, hopelessness, despair, and abandonment, while unearthing the rhythms of injustice, racism, and marginalization. Embodying the identifiably struggles of Latinas/os, Recinos's dexterous imagination paints for us a glimpse into the stubborn determination of this people to continue living in spite of divinely censured incalculable social and cultural forces of dehumanization."

—NESTOR MEDINA,
Associate Professor of Religious Ethics and Culture, Emmanuel College, University of Toronto

"Of the many important things these deeply felt poems accomplish—perhaps the most essential—is the view of White America they offer: the other side of America that's seldom seen with such bravado and honesty in American poetry; an immigrant Black and Brown America ripped open by White rage and indifference. Recinos's view of the role Christianity plays in all of this is equally profound and original. These are poems that needed to be written, truthful, often enraged, poems written by and for the soul. Amen.

—PHILIP SCHULTZ,
Founder, The Writers' Studio

"In Harold Recinos's luminous new book, *On the Sight of Angels*, the poignant features of everyday life serve as the ethical and aesthetic focus of his poetry. Recinos gleans love and meaning from the systematic fraying of experience. Chronicling the burdens of existence, each poem reflects on a tenacious will to life where connection and communion mitigate the vampiric violence of capitalism. What we experience as readers is the sheer brilliance of a poet committed to the vitality of ordinary existence, to the divinity of marginalized subjects, and to a revolutionary perseverance that brings light to the world."

—RICHARD PEREZ,
Director of U.S. Latinx Literature Minor, John Jay College of Criminal Justice, City University of New York

"To read Harold J. Recinos's *On the Sight of Angels* is to commit to listening deeply, openly, without shield or judgement. Each poem is an invitation to let go of the cacophony that surrounds us and listen to the heartbeat of those whose stories weave in and out of these pages; an invitation to let each story broaden our understanding of communion and acceptance. With the turn of the last page, I am reminded of how to live with others—not against each other."

—CLAUDIA ABURTO GUZMÁN,
Associate Professor of Hispanic Studies, Bates College

On the Sight of Angels

HAROLD J. RECINOS

RESOURCE *Publications* · Eugene, Oregon

ON THE SIGHT OF ANGELS

Resource Publications
An Imprint of Wipf and Stock Publishers
199 W. 8th Ave., Suite 3
Eugene, OR 97401

www.wipfandstock.com

PAPERBACK ISBN: 979-8-3852-3135-5
HARDCOVER ISBN: 979-8-3852-3136-2
EBOOK ISBN: 979-8-3852-3137-9

04/09/25

CONTENTS

THE WOMAN

how softly she spoke
ill at home from factory
work, telling a six year
old story of the ocean
surf on the island she
never again would see.
sweetly, she waited for
the child's smile, reaching
with a caressing hand and
recalling the day she was
lifted by her mother from
the sea.

DUTCH

imagine the young Puerto Rican
boy with a Dutch mother living
in the Bronx, walking sidewalks
blanketed by snow, hiding behind
parked cars to escape little Tito's
snowballs and left irrepressibly
laughing in a wonderland with
fire escapes flying all manner of
flags. imagine the sound of voices
in song, tambourines in the little
storefront church ringing glorias
to the God of the poor who chases
away the brutal cops, capricious
landlords and the lynching history
poured from school books into us.
imagine not a single child going to
school hungry, shooting dope, sent
to jail, brutally treated and told to
forget about freedom in a world in
which God only hears white lies
and more lies. imagine the Dutch
mother who changed over the years,
learned to speak Spanglish, still plays
with the neighborhood kids and feeds
them rice she calls honeycomb and
locusts while singing hymns no one
knows.

THE APARTMENT

I come from a place no one
knows by name, the kids play
on the street, swim in the East
river, barely smile in school,
make long lines in the summer
for a free meal, cool themselves
with pump water on hot summer
days, ride the subway downtown
to get a look at how white people
live, and visit the Valencia Bakery
to get a fresh smell of bread. I come
from a street that holds tightly to
dreams, mothers spend evenings
in bedroom shrine prayer and God
abandoned after a letter that fell to
earth from heaven was torn into
scrap paper. I come from a block
never imagined at the beginning of
the time, a neighborhood where
corners sigh and in secret moments
of laughter people talk about praying
the rosary, painting stories against
forgetting on the sides of subways,
resurrecting the dead and finding
a way to justly live.

ELEGY

there are no birds singing
on the branches of the bare
trees in front of the church
where Christ weeps about the
wreckage outside caused by
old men who think greed is
good. the liberty they seek is
to rob a nation without any
standing in the way, to name
exploitation, injustice, death of
the poor necessary adjustment,
fiction the face of truth and
God a name too weak in the
world to keep the exploited
from starving. old men in the
places of power dearest Blake
will never see heaven in a wild
flower, your eternity in an hour,
Christ in a stranger's face, nor
horror in the evil spoken by them
that send many into a lurid hole
of injustice. birds hardly sing any
more in a nation hardly recalling
the godly command to love one
another and not kiss executioners'
fetid hands.

GOD

the bells call the faithful
to devotion each week at
the unchanged ungodly
hour. the facts beyond
the church walls and stained
glass windows are oppressed
by Sunday morning preaching
somehow overlooking God's
claim on the world. in Gaza a
child looks for precious things
from her bombed house, a girl
in Texas two years away from
becoming a teen takes her life
fearful of being left alone if the
family is deported, thousands
of federal workers are now out
of work by order of the callous
minds that sumptuously dine and
talk about how to punish people
they despise. on Sunday stories
about the fear of kings are hardly
read and the near naked man that
dangled on a tree is never talked
about in terms of the fact that he
was monstrously lynched. perhaps,
next week the Word will make
its way into the dark noisy with
spoken prayers and we will see
the truth dripping into the world
from wounds.

ZELENSKY

it is easy to lie about
who started the rape,
massacres and killing
on invaded land. it is
easy to deny betrayal
and bully a Ukrainian
leader backed by his
entire nation to submit
to a Russian who makes
war crimes and slavish
surrender to power the
dinner conversation of
the felonious rich. it is
easy to make peace in
the name of extortion
listed among the earliest
of sins in the upside down
Bible held by an asshole
for a photograph. it is easy
to overlook the monstrous
noise of war and the killer
who orders it that will never
change and who celebrates
friends in the White House.
it is easy to see the faces on
men who derive pleasure from
the killing ordered by the
man once belonging to the
KGB and now a dictator with
a warrant for crimes against

humanity and some like those
the White House has pitched
for a grieving world to see.

DEAREST

I love you with the permanent
inexperience heaven alone can
guide, feel you closer than the
uncomplicated scent of flowers
in a vast garden drawing lovers
near and like Neruda alleged in
verse without knowing. I love
you on the shouting city streets,
the sidewalks with boarded up
churches, the bruised valleys on
another land and in the exhausting
places I need you. I first held your
hand in a world that was abysmally
divided in two, thousands of breaths
were swallowed by the earth and your
touch in all places saved me. I love
you without regret, in the best of times
and the worst of days and remembering
hours of laughter spoiling the struggle
of a sinister world.

TEARS

I was brought home from
the city hospital with tears
in my eyes by a Puerto Rican
mother who whispered to me
the days of suffering known
by the poor. when I learned
to read my eyes lingered on
the pages of her Bible shedding
tears that landed on the paper
staining it with the pain of the
witnesses abandoned by light
and godly words.

VODKA

sometimes I forget the years
of homelessness wandering
around troubled streets and
thinking about returning with
loneliness and fatigue to my
mother's apartment. I cannot
remember the feel of the living
room sofa, watching television
with time spreading across the
bruised block, waiting for my
brother to make it home before
the demons riding the streets on
brooms swept him into another
world. sometimes, I can hear
little Anthony and the Imperials
singing in my head like it was a
Saturday afternoon with mother
finding America. sometimes, I
understand too little about the
woman with braids, kids trying
to find the hoped-for land and
why I jumped without thinking
from roof-to-roof to escape the
dope fiend, Tarzan. sometimes,
I feel light and darkness greeting
me like it often did in the Bronx
when my mother put herself to
sleep with vodka and rum.

STREET KID

I was a homeless Puerto Rican kid
in the city and more invisible than
that girl who fell into a rabbit hole.
churches were never kind, the cops
that bothered to talk to me wanted to
take me home even though get out
was still ringing in my teenage
ears. I roamed the five boroughs,
traveled from sea-to-sea, then flew
across the ocean to the island owned
by Uncle Sam. I was the boy standing
in long queues outside of the skid row
shelters reserved for aged winos who
like me needed a bunk, a meal and
maybe a prayer. shrewd old winos
and junkies in those dumps told me
God did not create us all equal and
I didn't have a damn thing different
to say. my hands never had enough
of mission house donuts, candy bars
and playing deaf to the thousands of
questions thrown my way. my slight
hope one day found a home with a
family that had English names and
refused to leave me on the street for
dead. imagine the conversation for
several years at the table with a white
midwestern family with three young
kids and you will understand how I
taught them to speak Spanglish.

THE STATION

when you exit the subway
take Third Avenue until
you see the corner with
the church bell tower and
turn right walking some
three blocks to a set of old
grimy buildings with kids on
the stoop eating sugar cane
and talking Spanglish. here
is where the poor live, the
frail old men gather to play
dominos and drink beer and
single mothers who work hard
are glad summer winds blow
on them, while they do things
of little interest to the books
sold in university book stores
on the other side of town. go
into St. John's church to have
a look at the carved Saints, the
candles burning for them, and
the kneeling rail made of aged
wood that no longer hears white
prayers floating to heaven and
see the crucifix dangling behind
it that learned Spanish to make
darkness brighter.

SUMMER

from the fire escape on a hot
summer day, I looked at the
the fire hydrant being opened
with an ingenious hanger tied
to remnants of a broom stick
by kids. there were faces in the
scattered clouds floating south,
two lovers walked by holding
hands like the old couple living
on the ground floor apartment on
the way to the bodega. the only
sound of play was that of children
mischievously laughing expecting
to cool off in water sprayed from
the pump and nothing would keep
them from seeing glorious rainbows
in the gushing water that for a few
innocent moments would certainly
make the hot sun blush.

CHANGE

he used to dream of travel
to Paris with just a few bucks
in his pocket like Baldwin when
a young man, finding rooms in
cheap hotels and in the area of
the city full of artists. these days
his creativity is freed reading Go
Tell It on the Mountain, The Bluest
Eye and Bless Me Ultima mostly at
a sidewalk café on the block where
W. H. Auden lived. on a Third Street
rooftop in the pale light of a street
lamp reaching the fifth floor, for hours
he pondered the mutable things, the
beautiful and the bagel shop on First
Avenue owned by a Jewish lady that
called him darling. he was taught to
pray when a boy by an Irish Priest who
learned to speak Spanish and over the
years he has conducted conversations
of great length with the grace that fled
the earth when taken from the cross.
sometimes, alone in his apartment he
sang with Salsa artists on the radio and
he often made it to the spoken word
café to laugh with friends who never
pretended to be Angels. nowadays,
he thinks life moves along, while
enchanting youth too quickly flees.

SNOWY WINTER

it was one snowy winter night
in a crowded apartment with the
lights low when voices came to
me cloaked like poems, they called
to me from the street, the alleys,
rooftops, the church a few blocks
away and abruptly from Jewish
families in the tenement preparing
to move to a different side of the
city. I trembled trying to find a
way to respond to them, to figure
out their names, searching for paper
to scribble a few timorous lines in
an attempt to make sense of the
visit. they have never departed,
they perforate darkness with holes,
have made a home in the knot in
my throat, build balconies in the
deepest regions of my heart and
take my soul by the hand showing
it where to find the pure lines that
cannot rest until they break down the
doors that belong to those who never
listen.

COMMUNION

we spent the week becoming
in ways once imagined for
others, talking about streams
made in the desert, singing
of sun, water and a harvest
full of abiding life. we ended
the week able to see heaven
uncloaked in a rainbow of
dreams, we talked and laughed
about the chariots swinging low
for us and the Black hand of God
parting clouds blocking for too
long the abandoned love coming
for us. we ended the passage of
sacramental time with bread, drink,
song and repair surely more certain
the stony road by night or day will
make us complete. now, we give
thanks for the vast breath of God
giving us and the least in the world
an abundance of life for our souls
to grow deeper than the Jordan on
the way to a promised land.

UNACCOMPANIED

we are the forgotten children
of a wealthy world, jailed in
the slums, blamed for crimes
never committed, battered by a
system outlawing the color of
our skin and living nightmares
created on Wall Street. we are
unaccompanied minors crossing
borders to walk among the living,
write our names on barbwire walls,
weep about family separation and
find a promised land in this English
only country where Europeans first
arrived bearing names from a Spanish
colonial empire that kept our ancestors
chained. we are unseen kids suffering
like tortured Saints, who hide each day
from the white diggers of graves and in
our new broken English neighborhoods
ask why in a country declaring it is a city
on a hill it pledges to give us nothing more
than nightmares.

WORSHIP

the homily this Sunday morning
did very little to stir the dead in us,
nothing was gained from the lack of
exegesis and the truth that was to be
spoken this morning joined Lazarus
in sleep and maybe even dreaming he
was dead. we pleaded for heaven to
make an appearance in the sound of
words, for the infinite to move around
the sanctuary in a warming breeze, for
simple light to push through the stained
glass windows from whatever place it
began, and for the preacher to enchant
us with good news. I can tell you though
nothing was utterly lost in that rather ungodly
hour for the time came for breaking bread
that made us complete and filled us enough
to say a crucified God with unlimited love
who was lynched on a tree reminded us the
meek will inherit the earth and be lavishly
free.

HOSPITALITY

it is strange to understand
that in a space so dimly lit
you belong to hands that
reach for you, the candles
burning in the room with
a preacher finding a way
to make love speak, and
people roaming in a world
with strangers living with
changes. bring whatever
your soul possesses and
find peace in this church
before the daylight yields
to the dark. step into this
place where God is never
indifferent to the movement
of life and you will never be
unimportant for care. come,
let us speak to each other in
thick sentences about the One
who makes a way in the desert
and causes rivers to freely run
in them. today, let us cradle each
other at a wide table certain there
is enough and eager to be bread
and drink for others.

THE CITY

I miss the city in the summer
where pensioners with stories
settle for the day on benches
in a park, kids from the block
walk to Hunts Point for a long
morning fishing smiling at the
Mexican girls selling flowers,
grass pushes through cracks on
the sidewalk and the delicious
scent of bread exits the Valencia
Bakery fragrantly lingering in the
barrio universe like flowers found
unfaded on the street. I miss the
broken street light hanging in the
dark, the once upon a time kisses
that came from around the block
and the dreamy majesty of people
armed with restless hearts.

THE ORDERLY

I sing a few words of praise to
Miguel who went to work each
evening at the mental hospital
eager to be an orderly that gave
aid. he rode a bus thinking of
the thin mother of three he called
his girl, traveled to the white side
of town with watered lawns, flower
beds, and all the things that teased
delicate dreams. he wore a nurses
style uniform, cleaned pans, tucked
patients in bed and in the darkness
of the hospital ward sat in one corner
with a glowing lamp listening to a radio
chattering Pentecostal tongues like
tomorrow would never come. he
arrived in the city from a mountain
village wearing clothes that were
older than his years and soured by
hard work in sugarcane fields. he
spent his first days working in a
metal factory bending sheets and
year by year thought there had to
be something better. he endured
like the palm trees nearest to the
beach on his island of enchantment
until training to become an orderly,
working the crazy ward and with
his hard work that always felt the
presence of God was revered on

the block by little kids who lived
in the world that Judas negotiated
for petty change and called him by
a new name, Doc.

NAOMI

the old woman pulls a
two-wheel grocery cart
behind her to market
giving herself to thoughts
mumbled in a soft voice
on the sidewalk. you can
nearly see the recollections
brilliantly remaining on
her eyes of the man who
called her for more than
thirty years darling. the
word keeps her company
on lonely walks, in a dim
church and in late evenings
when it calls her name with
wonder in the darkness. the
old widow's heart is ablaze
still by the word darling and
the simple recollected term
will bless her endlessly while
her beloved is gone.

AGAIN

in the name of the messenger
of peace who so many believe
leaped into the world long ago,
these words again are lifted
for the dead and the criminal
sinner closer than ever to the
gates of hell. some cannot bring
themselves to pray a single word,
others will not lift their heads to
heaven and many cannot find a bit
of truth in the darkness that came
to a High School to swallow up
another group of kids. we pray
for those whose names are now
fading, with words no one ever
thought and with quivering lips
announcing the grieving day that
has leaned into us. in the name
of sorrowing hearts closer to the
discordant noises lingering in the
corridors of schools let us keep
from turning entirely away from
you in the world we have begged
God to change. in the name of the
thoughts and prayers for which a
country stands when will dead kids
who ran in corridors, crawled on
bellies and cried your name keep
you from listening to prayers from
those letting the gun have its say

counting the names of the dead?
thoughts and prayers will never
save a single child legislators allow
to prematurely die in this nation with
knees bending for the gun.

BROKEN

I carried a disobedient
soul across the country,
spoke with a wrinkled
tongue about elemental
things to rich kids living
in a beach house, spent
nights hushed on subways
going nowhere and could
not find comfort in prayer.
I wandered into areas where
they called me a dirty spic,
left scars written inside of
me like memories and year
after year they surface. I have
known more than nine lives,
dwelled in more than one
language, walked slowly
away from broken things
and sat on rooftops laughing
beneath full moons saying to
myself that in spite of many
descending days and tired nights
I love the broken meaning of
life.

THE BLOCK

come to the barrio streets
to hear music made in the
urban alleys called salsa
and rap, to see the dancing
and breaking that made its
way from the rice and bean
corners to Parisian Olympic
games. come see the people
thought foreigners in their own
country, see graffiti on backstreet
walls, the Cathedrals that just
learned Spanish, the storefront
churches praying for the entire
neighborhood, murals featuring
the Day of the Dead, the bodega
next to the synagogue built by the
Jews who fled Europe, the auto repair
shop on the avenue right in front of
Victor's building, the beauty salon
that teases hair until it surrenders,
the Brown, Black, Red, Yellow and
White humanity from Puerto Rico,
the Dominican Republic, Mexico,
Cuba, Chile, Honduras, Los Angeles,
and other parts. come hear the voices
of the women who escaped Central
American wars, gang violence and
need. come to the community known
simply as the block, where people
find thousands of ways to celebrate

the life often taken by guns, gangs, sickness and brutal ass cops. come get all the news overlooked by the evening broadcast, come and hear, come and see, come, and ask us for forgiveness.

MISSING

she departed the village to
become what is missing, an
absence closely known in a
home left along with a church
that stitched witnesses who
dared to break silence in public
squares. I went with her to
visit the free health clinic with
doctors who stumbled speaking
Spanish, did not wear overcoats
nor keep copies of the National
Geographic in a waiting room.
she spoke in a very low voice and
had a look in her dark eyes of a
young woman falling from the
flat world of toxic men. in the
consulting room keeping her
company my throat filled with
tangled words and I teared when
she told the medical student she
left the flesh of her flesh in Central
America against all odds and came
to get bandages for her breaking
heart.

PLUMES

the Peacocks roamed the night
on the mountain top calling to
each other loud enough to wake
the early morning Sun to display
their outspread colors. they kept
hotel guests from flawless sleep
announcing in the dark a time of
peace, an end to civil war, the rattling
of feathers and plumed heads held
high. these feathered creatures strutted
the length of night sometimes with open
feathers told stories to us of Angels they
have seen on hillsides gently singing
around hidden graves. they innocently
rove the grounds breaking the silence
with people unaware of the magic held
within. these peacocks keep us awake
tonight spilling sounds for words into
darkness and like the stony road they
will lead us away from sorrow to places
full of dreams.

BATTERY PARK

on the streets of this city, I
walked at night across dark
bridges, on cracked sidewalks
and spaces that were welcoming
and others not fitting. often, with
chills racing across my adolescent
skin from a jones I caught with other
Puerto Rican kids I felt the wind
blow my life down alleys littered
with yesterday's newspapers not
reporting any of the dreams the
poor held as they called America
home. on the streets, my days were
taken up by hell injected into a bony
teen arm sometimes in the name of
the Holy Trinity, friends dying and
children going hungry. I practiced
speeches on walks about rebelling
against school, uncaring churches,
prayers unanswered and junkies
unseen in houses of worship full
of long overdue good news. I walked
hopelessly for hours trying to find a
home, until reaching Battery Park to
sleep in Golgotha. decades later, with
no sign from above.

QUIETLY

we sat still in the dim sanctuary
without a word from any language
moving in us. we waited together
in silence for the divine mystery to
unfold, the one that strangely offers
to redeem the world in darkness and
that leaves us wondering about why
so little happens. we waited apart that
morning for a Holy experience to come
and linger the whole day with us on the
block, pulling coat racks in Manhattan
for pay, cleaning the offices downtown,
sitting in the classrooms where teachers
could not correctly say our names and to
erase the scars of empire that had nearly
vanished the last traces of light that dared
occupy our hearts.

RHAPSODY

I never heard theologians
talk about barrios where
people are unconcerned
with proving the existence
of the maker of things and
the Angels the old women
see. believe me when I tell
you that I learned to pray with
a Rosary around my neck, yelling
in four directions and dashing
into the basement of the big
Catholic church. I imagined
when a little boy on the block
chewing on sugar cane pigeons
flown by old Italian men on Papo's
roof were closer to God than
the cops at the 41st Precinct who
regularly tried to unmake us. one
day, I would like the lettered God
thinkers to visit a barrio to sing
harmonies in hallways with lost
kids and discover the dazzling
laughter of God pouring into the
streets from the broken English
lips heaven dressed in beautiful
dark skin.

TIME SPENT

I spent an afternoon on the island
with signs written in the blood of
the colonized who have been beaten,
drugged and jailed for more than a
hundred years by America. I talked
to a reefed merchant seaman with a
thick southern accent, living like me
at the Salvation Army mission home.
little did I know the good people looking
after us had me incarcerated in Old San
Juan existing in English and overhearing
outraged native speakers in a small plaza
next to a Catholic church talking about
who belongs and yanquis go home! I
talked with this Louisianan about the
God of his fathers who could not speak
a lick of Spanish, rewarded his world with
profits and never knew a day in chains. the
old man sweating manifest destiny sailed
on Gulf Oil tankers, was unfamiliar with
my America and the ways it was populated
with the ghosts of slaves and dark human
beings that boiled up in dreams. from time
to time, I think about the stranded sailor who
was the first white man in my fourteen years
of life that I ever talked with about empire
and the death that claimed the first seats on
the bus, train, plane and gun-ships delivering
obedience lessons to people denied a place each
day they wake up in the white world.

THE MASSACRE

when I left the overcrowded
city to travel mountain roads
leading to a remote village, I
passed extraordinary volcanoes,
fertile valleys, wrecked bridges,
and water filled craters made by
500-pound bombs where peasants
with unknown names were shot by
soldiers in the civil war. repeatedly,
I saw divine revelation in stones on
the side of the road, campesinos on
long walks to earn money for bread
yet demanding that their cries for plain
justice be heard, beautiful sound-proof
churches scattered on the landscape of
the ride, Ceiba trees pinching heaven
with stories about an indigenous broken
world and faces wherever I stopped for
a rest smiling with love. then, I arrived
one late afternoon to sit with the singular
survivor of a massacre that claimed the
lives of four of her children, a husband
and a village. I wept about the absence
of grace for the village poor holding the
trembling hand of the only witness to the
horrors denied by officials in her country
and mine.

SACRIFICE ALLEY

I woke one night in a storefront
watching an African God known
by the name Chango who was
dressed like a woman in a white
cotton dress that danced to the
sound of drums men played. she
could read minds in the room,
lift the weary hearted better than
Lazarus from the dead. she knew
everyone in the space since the
days mosquitos chased them in
jungles, the hours they suffered
hunger and thirst in deserts or the
time they were told you're the biggest
problem of the 21st century in these
United States. I believed her words
were more than superstition, spoke
to the lashing whips scarring backs,
and questioned why an African God
was not good enough for bread, wine
and hymns. I smiled when Chango
came to stand in front of me and
recalled this deity was not eager to
sacrifice the children of the poor to
the wolves on earth.

BUS STOP

life is short was the line
playing me on the way to
the school bus stop to drop
my daughter. my life has been
to death valley and back more
than a thousand times though
I only tell my children of the delicious
ways the world has held me by the
hand to keep me from dying in small
doses. my daughter shared a few
words on the drive that morning that
made me weep. out of the blue, the
girl said, "you have to live for a long
time dad, I don't want to be in the
world without you." I said, "Darling,
I promise to keep saying life is beautiful
for a long time and even God in endless
time will not be closer than me."

KITE-FLYER

he loved going to the rooftop
when visiting his divorced
mother to fly kites high above
the telephone wires with old
brand name sneakers dangling
on them like a sign of community
wealth. the diamond shaped kites
he made flew the conduits of wind
on bright Saturday mornings and it
made him smile like a boy with a
grip on reality. I never did forget
the day the paper winged things
with a long tail flew it appeared a
mile high over tenement roofs doing
aerial somersaults like Jimmy who
practiced gymnastics at Monroe High
School like the rich white kids. he flew
these tissue paper and bamboo things
like they delivered him to another place
eager for him to float up and up to feel
the wind caressing his face until heaven
came nearer.

HAYMARKET

in a bar on Eighth Avenue
patronized by people loathed
by potbellied men and women
who are adored in church, Gypsy
once the star of La Cage aux Folles
in Los Angeles and a performer in
many Mel Brooks movies talked of
being made famous far beyond the
night she was introduced by Milton
Berle. Gypsy loved telling the audience
Chita Rivera the Broadway star
named her. you may recall Gypsy appeared
with Miley Cyrus on the annual MTV
special glamorously dressed at eighty-five
for her female impersonation act or perhaps
you caught her playing alongside of Jane
Fonda and Jeff Bridges in the box office
film, *The Morning After*. patrons in the
honky-tonk bar laughed when Gypsy said
she borrowed eyelashes from the fabulous.
before TikTok, email, or Instagram Gypsy
did a drag show in a cabaret attracting big
money audiences in awe of her fancy ways
and glamorous dresses. I wish my dear friend
who spent many nights in her criminalized
world had not drunk himself to death just to
drown the sounds of the world's gay hate.

CHANGE

I have grown cold to the church
with tarnished Christians soothed
in their favorite pews by prayers
quick to wound those on the other
side of its doors. I have cooled to
the stout Methodist pastor with no
heart for ministry with the Brown
children of God, deaf to the loud
shouting streets and pressed every
Sunday with well-paid dreams. I
am tired of Sunday morning pious
confessions by those quoting the
Bible and offended by the sick, the
weak, the widows, women, the poor
and same sex human beings in love.
I am impatient with worshipers who
have forgotten scripture says in many
ways love the vulnerable more than
candles in church.

PEACE

there is a monument on the road
leading to the airport in El Salvador
known as the monument to peace
and it has the biblical verse on it,
"peace be onto you." Jesus made
of bronze and discarded bullets is
signaling the V sign with one hand
and holding a dove in the other. the
monument was placed there two
years after the Peace Accords that
ended a brutal civil war was signed
and in time for the fifth Central American
Games. now, kids often visit the spot
to skateboard, young adults exercise,
and others to sit with Jesus thinking
of peace. years ago, I took a photo
on that spot keeping it in the drawer
of a desk I found on the streets in
New York to remind myself of the
bloody civil war fields, the illegal
jails, tortured friends, buried family
and motives for peace. often, I wish
the Black and Brown quarters I call
home had churches collecting guns
to melt into sculpted monuments
to peace.

EPIPHANY

we climbed the mango tree to
sit on the upper branches beside
an ant mound that was home to
these six-legged creatures returning
from a day of foraging and many
things yet undone. these horned
wanderers knew their way around the
grass where they were blown at times
by strong winds to places not ever
visited. one came walking across
the branch with a cookie crumb from
Mrs. May's kitchen like the treats she
took to the Kingston market to make a
few shillings. I could almost hear the
tiny creature speaking to me. then, I had
an epiphanic moment in the mango tree
realizing these ants roam the world with
no word for God and they have traveled
with us from the beginning.

MULLING

God a poet said speaks to us
in the making then spends the
years mutely present enjoying
I presume the longing that drives
us to seek. we have wondered
about the sentiment whenever the
executioner with yellowing rope
has come to the neighborhood in
a business like quest for innocent
and crimeless necks. we have all
asked how often does the Creator
declare I did not see and I cannot
hear the teeming words of sorrow
from the blessed who are vulnerable
and growing in bitter disbelief. in
assaulting times, I assume the contented
have reason to travel smelling heavenly
lavender in fields hidden from the poor
and convincing themselves God is near.
still, in the dark places familiar to me
people schooled on hope often think
divine silence is a waste.

CALM

send me a feather from an
Angel's wing a little stained
by everyday life, tell me you
found it up the street by the
corner where the wind runs
loose and you even heard the
innocent souls sing. tell me the
prayer you most often repeat,
how you shed tears when the
words leave your lips and how
certain you are that God knows
each time you start it. share once
again, the story about the angelic
visitor who sat in the corner of
your room with a hairless round
face spreading her wings like the
pigeons that play in puddles after
rainfall and in that calm time how
you learned all there is to know of
light.

BARCELONA

the tabletop at Las Ramblas
covered by a white cloth
with faded red stains from
spilt wine is surrounded by
Catalan, Spanish, German,
English, French, Portuguese
and a few languages from
the other side of the earth.
on the feverish street there are
no signs of ancient ruins, no
sound of air raids Langston
said were worse than screams,
just a bustle of people touching
thousands of spots and enchanting
the streets with commotion from
far and near. I sat with friends at
a sidewalk café wondering whether
or not dreams were on the menu, the
waiters kindly smiled saying they
had aged here. the museums in the
city kept their memories, Gaudi put
them on the walls of his Cathedral
and Placido Domingo delivered them
singing the aria from the third act of
Puccini's Tosca with viewers imagining
it without end.

SPEAK

let me say in Spanglish
in this country with the
gun for religion, on the
earth and never heaven,
thoughts and prayers appear
like hollow speeches sticking
on walls like crap. from school,
to pulpit, prison to workplace,
corner to government hall, no
jolt of hate will displace the
fierce love on the tough faces
of my beloved people known
by the places walked by Romero,
King, Hughes, Neruda, Lorca,
Mistral, Piñero, Pietri and others
kept in cadenas until the end. let
me say the wails from every grave,
the cries of those once enslaved, the
school-boys Martin and Toledo who
will never again play have witnesses
to interfere with America's charred
kindness.

SALVATION

I was called out by God beneath
the distant stars in a cracked junkie
world that knew more of hell than
gathering by a stream in Eden. the
shadows were never lifted from the
streets familiar to me, the blood stained
places always unchanged and monstrous
habits created memories that made me
wonder how anyone is created in a divine
image on earth. I thank God for lifting
the veil over my eyes to disclose a mystery
allowing me to know a crucified carpenter,
the Word made flesh, a stranger who weeps
for the poor, teen junkies, homelessness and
those praying at the graves of the prematurely
departed. I thank God for feeling love holding
the widow Lela's hand, seeing heaven on the
hopscotch sidewalk and finding Eden dressed
like colorful dreams.

THE FUNERAL

the city cried out his name
for the first time when the
young man died. the block
was panic stricken and most
everyone had a huge knot in
the throat and misty eyes for
they would no longer hear the
Spanglish jokes the kid told
no matter where he happened
to be. the little church that held
his funeral did not shush the dark
for those who attended the service
to get a last look, the priest doing
his best to let scripture lift a room
of sunken hearts pretended God
was preparing a letter of explanation
to everyone. for weeks, nights of
hanging on the corner wept.

THE ACCIDENT

the Cathedral bells rang like
sirens gliding down the street
hurrying to an accident where
strangers inquisitively took time
to find each other. on the sidewalk,
the elderly watched children jumping
rope in front of the building with a
few Jewish families that never left
the block and they rescued each other
from the ticking clock on Southern
Boulevard promising daily to sing
one day a last time. today, we will
catch prayers in the bodegas, find
them on shelves and in store aisles
where the wounded shop. the buses
passed the Cathedral slowly and among
the faces full of judgement an old woman
with a black head scarf kneeled beside
a boy hit by a car pleading his cause to
a Spanish speaking God.

SEASONS

to everything I read there is a
season like a time to weep and
another to laugh, a time to keep
silent and speak. these are the
most curious words that creeped
out of the Bible I found on Ma's
Holy altar. the words have made
me think for years about expendable
people in the barrio, criminalized for
being poor and viewed unworthy of
love, laughter, attention, or tears. when
a boy roaming the city, I recall standing
on the subway platform on Simpson
Street looking around at adults with
determination on their Black and Brown
faces feeling convinced they knew more
about living in different seasons than me.
I confess being puzzled to this very day
about why the longest season known on
the streets of beloved broken-back people
is death that wails like a Northern wind
just before claiming another life.

MUSIC

it was just a few minutes after
eleven and Papo came down
to sit on the stoop with his new
transistor radio. the sidewalks
were slowly going silent, a few
stray dogs disappeared in a glum
alley, and delightfully the show
loved by every kid on the stoop
started to salsa music that found
a refuge in this old city just like
the Guatemalan family that fled
a civil war. no one was disturbed
by the music emptying into the
night like spirits from enchanted
land faraway. each melody carried
stories told by these kids who loved
staying up all night until the morning
traffic started on the avenue. on the
block, the kids growing in two languages
listened to the radio blurting Spanglish
and labeling them brown beautiful.

SUBWAY

the subway ride does not
have the incessant babble
it did before the invention
of the cellphone. the city
still moves underground in
it but people mostly stare at
screens drawing open curtains
that give a peek on the lives of
others courtesy of TikTok. the
blonde girl wearing headphones
is lost in what I can imagine to
be a surreal musical playground
imaged like a world that never
hurts. a young man enters the
half-filled car, dressed in black
with a sign reading help, jobless,
homeless, orphaned, hopeless and
hungry. the lights are not bright for
him on Broadway like they are for
the family visiting from Cleveland
and heading back to their downtown
hotel, after a day at the Bronx Zoo.
in the far corner of the subway car,
an old man with a drooping head is
completing a paper puzzle dreaming
likely of the coffee and buttered roll
waiting for him at the next stop, love
given from heaven or another
night on the IRT outing.

POLICE BRUTALITY

the list of names for the gone
is longer than yesterday and
too long for those who were
unmade by police violence not
more than hours ago. every time
a cop kills a Black and Brown boy
we hear let us pray, white society
blots it out, and too many of us just
shout this has got to stop. I can hear
forty-six-year-old George screaming
with his Black soul I cannot breathe
with a cop's knee on his neck taking
him out without apology. sometimes,
I dream of throwing one of these errant
white cops to the ground to give him a
taste of the kind of treatment they give
dark-skinned bodies. how many more
lives are going to be ended for America
to stop making us take a last gasp for no
crime committed save that by the blue
with a badge. Black and Brown mothers
ask God to protect their kids though for
hundreds of years the supremacists have
shot, stomped, crushed, and dangled us
from trees. these racist bastards who
keep us crying with maggots consuming
what is left of our hearts listen to this we
matter and the sirens next time will
be coming for you!

EXQUISITE

life is beautiful like
shared bread on the
evening steps of the
old tenement where
grandmothers sit at
windows watching
children on the street
play. life is fine on
the rooftop where Joey
goes to fly kites and the
five floors above ground
feel a little nearer to God
in heaven. life is exquisite
happiness and light just like
the love in your eyes never
old.

THE FIRE

the morning after the fire
in the tenement on West
Farms Road they sat giving
thanks for the child who asleep
when smoke filled the crowded
apartment, survived. the fire this
time was set by an angry old man
who entered an apartment through
an open fire escape window belonging
to his estranged daughter. we watched
the crackling flames without offering
prayers, saw the father who set the
blaze tumble down the steps with the
cops behind him, and an old woman who
lived in the building walked out of the
tenement fumbling tears. in the ruins of
the residences, with food tasting like smoke
crosses were in the eyes of mothers, scared
children and old men with time left to play
dominoes in an alley sharing ale and laughter.
they spoke loudly using two European languages
settled in them like countries stumbling before
collapse.

RIVER WALK

I walked with you along the
East River gently stroking
your heart with whispered
words and believing myself
in the tiny crowd of strollers
touched by endless love. my
darling, I will walk with you
until every lover chants beneath
the moon that blushed above this
river when it saw the first lovers
on earth. I will never wonder
what comes next, fear valleys
of the dead or stop pushing back
darkness coming around to lead
me astray. I will love you by day
and night, the very way God lets
me and in the places imagined at
time's end.

MADRE

you can see her on the
stoop eating quenepas
pulled from a brown bag
one at a time. her son got
the treat of Spanish lime
for her after spending a whole
day living in English at the
public school. you can see
they taste delicious, they wipe
away island tears and lift her
from the last round of a hard
day of work. the warmth of
the whistling wind on a late
Spring day, pigeons dancing
on the sidewalk and the treat
given to her by the boy made
the time the best stoop sitting
mother's day.

ELEMENTS

I saw the moon lean over
the edge of the roof that
evening like the old lady
in the third-floor apartment
looking out of her window.
it cast shadows the length
of the sidewalk, roamed by
single-mothers in love with
their kids, winos stumbling
out of the alleys and aging
couples taking one step at a
time. I heard a rooster crow
in the basement of building
1203 behind the Super's door,
ate food from a Chinese take
out box with Carmen Julia on
the stoop, thought of people
wandering the streets in rags they
had not changed for months, and
thought Jesus should be depicted
on Crosses in such rags, rather
than a loin cloth.

NIGHT SKY

just before midnight the
last bus rushes past

the front of the church
building making glass

windows shiver. when
kind passenger eyes

come into the shadow
of the darkened stoop

you welcome them like
the stars embraced in an

evening sky. you often wait
beautifully at that hour for

the little kids from Avenue
D with tears and wounded

voices who come to sit. they
tell stories of being blamed

for faults in the neighborhood
where clothes hang from rope

between ramshackle tenements.
you know them quite well like

the many others who stand on
corners waiting for the light

to change that says walk and
allowing you to lift your eyes

grateful for the kind message
guiding you like the sermons

given in that tiny church that
never seem to end.

HOME STREET

this morning, I walked down
the street to the corner to wait for
the bus that made desperate stops
along the avenue to reach passengers
with conjured visions. I boarded
the machine still believing life is more
beautiful than any sorrow lingering in
Bronx air, the vanishing hours familiar
to the kids questioning lessons in public
schools excluding them and the shoe
boxes the Puerto Rican widows keep
in closets with faith saved from another
life. I listened to the noisy city talking
loudly into one ear, thought about the
idle factories no longer cradling working
class desires and those living in abandoned
buildings that have found many ways to
explain everything. my part of the city
is near to the East River that flows below
a park with baseball fields where lovers
go to share kisses. I loved roaming a patch
of bushes by the river inhaling a honey
suckle scent still coming to me in sleep
and when I chance a visit to the Home
Street tenement.

WAITING

one Spring night, after the
raucous city bus dropped
silent workers at a stop on the
endlessly woeful boulevard,
the restaurant at the foot of
the subway stair's entrance
with rousing coffee filled with
people planning futures away
from these streets named in honor
of well-known killers called in
American school books, heroes. I
lived beyond the bus stop with my
broken English people kept out of
fine print college books. I thought
high-brow intellectuals must like
overlooking the world of the poor,
the vulnerable and strangers and
they preferred to talk with each
other concerning made up shit
about life in the ghetto.

HOTLINE

I remember the days sitting
beside a telephone in a barrio
project talking to Puerto Rican
kids in Spanish, broken English,
and the language of the street who
tossed nights and felt their throats
jammed with colonial gibberish
and the usual Christian drivel
ignorant about the color of their
lives. they wept for the country
that found many ways to aspire
for domination in the world their
parents fled, the bloody wealth
white America insisted God had
confided in it, and the conspiracy
of barbarism paraded in schools
and on barrio streets slowly and
occasionally rapidly swallowing
them into early graves. often, I
listened to the words they poured
into my ear, denounced the savage
hours shackling them, the discourse
of equality and God turned into an
excuse for violence and asked like
a child who lost everything for them
to be set free.

HOMEGROWN

the night I crawled into the
Hudson Hotel the block in
the Bronx disappeared, the old
men forgotten by the country
they militarily served who shined
shoes on the corner evaporated
like dew on Spring grass in Crotona
Park, Spanish names slipped into a
cultural coma, and a drag queen
who lived in the room next to the
one I rented held my hand saying
welcome, kid. despite being shot
at on the block, I was afraid of
sleeping in the dark and whenever
I dared close my eyes shadows in
human form roved the room cursing
in my thirteen year old ears. kids in
that hotel were never looked for and
their words unheard in church, school
and homes. the place still haunts me,
like the days of not remembering the
sound of my late brothers voice, the
tenderness of a mother, the bond of
a father and a place called home. I
confess home is a four letter word
that in the bitter dark of the Hudson
Hotel still in me is charged with the
fault of those long gone.

DUST

I have visited cemeteries
in every season hearing the
words ashes to ashes, dust
to dust, and unsure these
young boys gone would
find a resurrection. I have
listened to religious words
while Salvadoran children
in cheap boxes were lowered
into holes with family twisted
in knots as light vanished
in them. the words spoken
in those places were always
the Spanish thought political
resistance in America and no
less a spiritual wail by these
tombs. I have cried for people
who harvest coffee, sugarcane,
cotton, and corn. prayed with
those working hard in a foreign
language to pay funeral home
debts. now, I must ask does God
feel the deaths of these innocent
kids?

MOUNTAINS

the land is adorned with
mountains majestic and
silent as the first light of
dawn guides them into a
new day. listen to songs
from the birds who live
there, the stories shared
on trees covering these
giants, the truths scattered
on stones bearing witness
to the keepers of forests
and rivers on the beautiful
earth and find your place
in their mysteries.

BLESSINGS

if you could dream in
dark-skin near doors
that give you passage
to other countries, to a
different movement of
time, to the place doves
hatch from stones and no
rules of division apply,
you would not miss hope
moving her lips to send
you the sound of deepest
faraway love. if you could
hold fast to dreams older
than your childhood starts,
nourished by a mysterious
bread of justice and basked
in anonymity you would be
closer to the Black and Brown
blessedness of earth and closer
to healing the white nationalist
condition.

THE BOY

the first boy on the block
to visit his divorced mother
was Joseph. he lived miles
away with a man no one had
ever seen though his father's
name was scrawled on a wall
of a building on Hoe Avenue.
every Friday the boy got off
a bus whose last stop was in
front of the building where his
mother lived. he left the transport
spitting prayers, cursing heaven
and playing with a K-55 knife
he carried in a front pocket of
fine trousers. he was always
the best dressed boy on the block,
wearing pepper silk trousers, nice
firsthand shoes, Alpaca sweaters
and smelling like a forest from a
world not damned. he loved his
mother who got sick and passed
away prematurely from a condition
medicine could have cured were
she not too poor to acquire it. he
insisted death had called out the
wrong name when his mother left
this world to become dust. the boy
changed till the day dope whisked
him away too on a rooftop that all
say should not have been.

MOLTMANN (1926-2024)

you assured us of the message
of a Crucified God wrapped in
the promises of resurrection for
a divided world. for many years,
we listened attentively to stories
shared from the darkest edges of
history and the places where the
cross pleads life for the innocent,
the vulnerable, the weak, the poor,
the loathed and all the conjurors of
hope. you reminded us not to be so
laden by philosophy to miss the Word
made flesh in the world and in all that
is. now, doctor, we turn conversation
to your departure, the spirit you leave
us, the surprises and feasts yet to come
where we will laugh, cry and eat with
you the sweet bread of life.

THE CUT

life is on the other side of
the bars consistently keeping
step with others on the block
chasing equality. life is a full
day of truth no crime on any
crooked sidewalk can silence,
distant from the vengeful God
of the storefront church, never
scented like the basement rot
or in need of the pretty stained
glass windows of a church. life
is children at play rapidly running
around corners, Spanglish worth
naming, the apartment where the
widows gather on Friday night to
say the Rosary, prayers meant to
gain a heavenly audience and the
next week cleared of nails. life is
a mass of time chiseling its way to
trembling souls, history written by
Wilfredo the elevator operator who
works downtown and the dream of
a colorful altar cloth with the names
of the damned.

THE STAND

on the side of the
road, the highway
stand has gathered
a small crowd, they
have come to drink
their fill of coconut
water. a loud clear
bark from a dog is
heard coming from
a field, heat rising on
sugarcane fields stretches
into the hobbled distance.
the standing crowd sipping
the refreshing potion on the
side of the road was like a
printed page of news, blessed
by a light drizzle dampening
young iguanas darting on the
side of the road.

FLOWERS

child, go to the corner for
flowers for your mother's
apartment, make sure the
scent is strong like fresh cut
mangos. imagine the Mexican
girl selling them on the corner
is close to renting a storefront
to open a florist shop in front of
which her friends will come to
dance on the sidewalk. let your
eyes open wide on the way home
with the bouquet, make the sign
of the cross when you pass the
church on Intervale, greet old
women wearing black dresses,
and stand quietly before your
aging mother to hand her the
many petaled surprise and wait
for her tongue to remember what
to say. you may hear tonight that
one day when this woman was a
little girl flowers grew on the side
of a mountain and in a small garden
she strengthened her slender arms
that hold you.

DRIFTING

tonight, you drifted across
the corridor of the house
holding the journal that is
with you no matter where
you roam to soothe troubled
times. this little book whose
blank pages you fill listens
to what is on each scribbled
page and leads you back to
the place peculiar psalms are
read out loud by your mother.
dear son, last night disquieting
news was set aside when we
laughed loudly in Spanish at
a dreamless country refusing
to understand us and unable to
confess we belong. son, you
are home, our place for a heap
of living for you to write about
and sing!

PSALM 13

I weep for my country
whose future is dripping
from my brown cheeks to
earth. you can see another
history extinguishing lights
in the windows and advancing
toward ruin. I am a stranger
to my country who was born
in a dirty hospital at the edge
of an affluent city that feeds on
the penniless and weak. I cry
out in the crippling silence of
my rejected people, for signs
from a God who only hides and
is far too silent. I plead an end
to inhumanity, the narrowing of
perspective and the near dead
American dream. how long Lord?
tell me?

SILENCE

the church bells in mourning
said life had nothing more for
the people who worked in
the factories under the load
of owners' greed who had
falling skin and bones ready
to drop into the earth. we
went to kiss them farewell
taking turns tossing bits of
dirt unto beds of silence. a
few of us thought thousands
of years are in those graves
where there is no air, no light
and no God fumbling in the
dark. we whispered to each other
that departed friends had more
treasure than the wealthiest in
the city in dreams they cherished
on earth's time silence in the old
apartments is painful now that the
light of so many has slipped over
the edge and priests too often have
not more than well-practiced words
to share.

DAUGHTER

my daughter sits with me
in the afternoon, light shines
through her eyes even after
the sun retreats. she opens
a page from her journal to
share with her preacher Dad
notes scribbled by hand and
attached to her heart that is
filled with love. she spends
time lighting bonfires in the
places too dark for the least
among us and I love the way
she is fierce when storms in
the world are wailing about
women's rights denied. she
reminds me the sky changes
colors routinely and grace
is abundant in the world for
those who see. I pray giving
thanks for her sweet disclosure
of the meaning of things and
for spreading her dreams at the
feet of the earth.

LORD'S PRAYER

it is impossible to forget
the prayers of peasants
living in fear crying to
you for Judgement Day
to lastly come. they pray
for your reign to enter,
daily bread and shielding
from penniless labor and
soldiers guns. they forgive
each other their debts and
wonder will you pardon
the uniformed men who
slaughter them, the evil
services of killing they
deliver to quiet children
who will not be here to see
your power and glory on
judgement day. I heard them
crying in a world serving
blasphemy, mercilessness
and hate. I heard a mother
who lost four children scream
at you in heaven doubtful of
your goodness though her grief
was not for lack of love in the
promises of heaven. I pray good
Lord for you ask this woman
for forgiveness!

AWAY THE DARK

even in darkness we walk
knowing that with just a few
more steps it will be possible
to create light, nothing can keep
us from finding candles lit in the
spaces filled with howling, even
the dust on the stony road shines
in the dark like a sign of coming
brightness making things happen
and wiping away tears. we are
children of light you see, those
who stroll beneath a canopy of
love, unafraid to gather whatever
glitters in a broken world in need
of fixing.

SCHOOL YARD

on the schoolyard kids
are in motion beneath a
teacher's watchful eye.
they holler in Spanglish,
or city slang and not one
grammar lesson dares take
up the fun. the girls at one
end play hopscotch and jump
rope, the boys are slapping a
pink Spalding against walls
and games are lugged for a
good hour behind a chained
linked fence. in one corner, a
little boy surrounded by friends
pulls from a pocket a postcard
with the image of a beach sent to
him by his abuela across the sea
and he gets a closer of view of love
sent by a wise and gentle Brown
aging woman reaching into a place
she has never visited.

THE PARADE

in the early hours the pigeons
danced pointing us to the wide
Avenue for the quiet stroll to
Central Park to the meadow
with late Spring daisies pushing
up and unleashed dogs catching
frisbees after chewing on biscuits
and lapping water. it is the place
bringing hope to the Puerto Rican
Day parade with San Juan imitators
handing out shots of rum, while the
trampled chilling beneath splashes of
warm daylight welcome slow marchers
on the Avenue breaking shackles for
other lives. not a single sour note was
heard played by the salsa band moving
north on the route. they performed for
people bending into the light like the
boys and girls full of cheer who dry
wet hair in the wind after a day of
playing in an illegally opened fire
hydrant.

JOHN THE BAPTIST

they came to the sandy
shore to open their piercing
eyes for a close look at each
other in the name of the milk
and locust eating Baptist from
ancient days who inspires the
persevering have a midnight soul
washing. we dropped into the
water backwards three times
and heard words from the dead
arriving in flight like pelicans
calling to us. there was drumming
on the sandy beach, rejoicing for
miles, prayer from the penitent,
shouts in Spanish and Spanglish
from the colonized and many acts
of faith. a Brown God touched us
in Atlantic sea like enslaved ancestors
recalled loaded into the belly of a ship
named Jesús. yes, there is something
here like redemption, a sweet destiny
of freedom and it will eagerly drag us
soon to heaven.

THE BEACH

I look east to see yellow
rising bright and feel a
salty gust of wind. the
last stars slipped away,
waves beat against the
unforgettable sands, lovers
stroll holding hands and
kiss in sight. remember
this place started without
us in paradise and now
its undivided light comes
for us with the angled spirit
of ancestors pouring dreams
into hearts. come, enter the
Borinquen sea to find what
you wanted to feel in books
and scribble in ancient sand
words about what it means to
be at the edge of paradise.

THE FOUNTAIN

the pigeons are gathered
around a Spanish water
fountain, a few dancing
by the feet of a German
traveler holding a three
month old girl tenderly
in his arms. he is singing
softly to her, a boy with
him tosses seeds at birds
and the genius of love in
this old city is the woman
who looks upon them with
a tender smile.

THE DRINK

beside the blue waters
of an old sea we drank
a coconut potion on an
island owned by Uncle
Sam which is a sweet home
to exiles living on it and to
those in one State or another
suffering injury. we are exiles
of lost love, sofrito people,
faces in the rain forest wearing
the smiles of ancient cultures.
today, bad times nonetheless
have been thrown to the depths
of the ocean so we can laugh in
Spanish and sing ageless songs.

ELDERLY

growing into the days
of elapsed youth, edging
toward more narrow time,
making gestures from time
to time to nobody present,
giving thanks for memories
untouched by grey worn-out
matter, talking fondly with
family and friends who make
unannounced appearances in
the oddest places and in dimly
lighted hours glad for each
breath of life. love carries
us through each day, it is truly
delicious to recall our name, to
stroll in a crowded marketplace,
to jump across vast territories
online to joyfully hear voices
of kids raised and even to gather
losses like beautifully scented
flowers that laugh us into old
age.

MISUNDERSTOOD

eternity is not well understood
for it has passed by us more than
once, first carried to the block by
a northern wind, poured from the
sky like a river and always distanced
from the small things giving us joy
without crooked lines. a few of us
set out with compasses in search of
trees with green branches in Crotona
Park, believing the dreams of the old
women on the block would be hanging
uncrumpled on them, carrying written
prayers in the pockets of cheap pants
and letters stuffed into a bottle from
the children who lived in the building
where Manny overdosed his way out
of being shipped to Viet Nam to fight
and die like other poor kids. eternity
changed since the day it was forgotten
that in the beginning was the word with
a heavenly being who cared about us.
perhaps, we should climb to the roof
to conjure new gods pleading for them
to disclose divine secrets to end all fear
of nothingness.

OVERDOSE

on a hot summer night, the
same year Tito was stabbed
on Southern Boulevard, I
thought it unbearable to see
the next hour and pleaded
with God to let me find the
morning again to begin to
kick a jones that bargained
with the devil to keep me
enslaved. death was close to
me like a July scorching sun,
cold chills said I needed a fix,
the memory of a knife buried
in my wrist by a desperate junkie
too vivid, and flesh and blood
threatened the end. on the rooftop
floor next to me was the boxed set
J. R. R. Tolkien's Lord of the Rings
that traveled with me to more than
one middle earth and I shouted to
heaven something about letting me
live to at least finish reading it. each
night, I sang alone swing low sweet
chariot, hoping God would send one
to carry me home and away from the
potter's field.

4TH OF JULY

freedom is a thing
celebrated for years
but saturated today
with distractions
about the future. it is
a thing for centuries
glad to sing white on
white anthems that a
worn out lost cause will
never keep from rising in
every color that stomped
the land from shining seas
to exploding days of purple
mountain majesties. freedom
is more woke than fireworks
rousing the nation once again
from sleep.

THE LINE

there comes a time on the
way to the border that you
think of guards with guns
on watch, the rules learned
about how to cross, places
you may not see again, how
to become invisible to people
doing whatever necessary to
stop marching history and
flowers already dead that you
carried from home. you have
heard the crossing will do little
to change your messy origin in
the world that waits for you that
the rich owning men use well to
condemn you to the painful labor
required by them and called the
rule of law. you will not have
any time to rest and days will be
avoiding Migra workplace raids
or waiting for God to arrive to
help you vanquish understanding
too little. there will be times you
will feel sick hearing stories about
border crossings and you will close
your dark eyes to imagine thousands
of candles lighting the pitch-black
heavens spelling your name.

THE FIT

there is one key that fits
the door you have never
knocked on in the building
at the very top of the sloping
hill, a woman hides behind
tattered drapery covering a
window and it is useless to
ignore the hours she spends
behind the pane staring at
the street. behind the door,
in locked rooms inside of her
where life she would tell you
is difficult to prove she prays
at an altar trying to unmask the
gods that come around the block
disguising themselves as ordinary
people without a penny in the bank
to their name. the noises from the
busy street cannot enter the space
she calls her own and they never
interrupt her conversation with a
collection of Catholic Saints on a
dresser top held in a language that
many would like dead.

NICARAGUA

today, something unexpected
occurred at the airport in the
presence of an airline agent
who was checking me in for
a Nicaragua trip. the news
left me breathless, I made a
few different faces and felt
like a wall had converged all
around me. my papers were in
order and my passport begged
for a trip to the land that was once
a place of Christian revolution.
the agent looked into my eyes and
said the Nicaraguan government
disallows my entrance given my
history of writing about respect
for human rights. the initial words
made me quiver thinking that there
would be no talk with others about
peasant dreams keeping watch for
a new world and not a single thing
said about justice binding itself to the
poor who have been hurt too long. the
darkness was like a blanket pulled over
my eyes, while ashes from a different
time was being used now to barricade
the door to truths that matter.

THE HAND

consider the hand that has
traveled taking the time to
carefully write the world it
journeyed, scribbling stories
from many places, rescuing
nostalgia, the slightest images
of love and everything that is
believed to return to simple
dust. consider its description of
cities set high on the hills like the
color of children's eyes, the ways
it keeps experiences of care and
is always present to gently lift one
up. the hand that moves is a sign
of words, the flesh and bone that
is caressing, holding, desiring and
creating. shall we ever entirely
reach an understanding of the many
words it leaves us written in pencil
and the precious labor of love. the
hand offered us flowers like elderly
ladies who sit at the base of a train
station offering rushed pedestrians
the signed flower held for too long
by wrinkled fingers.

DOVE

I looked out the window and a
dove was perched on a tree
branch. it overlooked a colorful
butterfly no doubt on its way
to Michoacan. it was not the
dove evoked by the Psalmist,
the feathered creature of new
beginnings mentioned in the Bible,
the winged Spirit of God talked
of in the Talmud, a goddess from
Canaan or the bearer of an after
flood message. this creature was
no more than a beautiful bird that
entered my life for a few moments
of rest from her wanderings. I can
tell you she sat sweetly on a tree
and made it a Holy.

THE DICTATORS

fields are saturated with
the scent of decaying flesh
and on the hillsides hidden
from eyes the bones of the
missing. around a dinner
table the dictators lift their
wine glasses finely praising
evil they call good though
the dead speak against the
ruthless and nauseating times
they leave us. these autocrats
have decided to holiday in the
stench of their worlds, drive nails
into cheap wood coffins and
are glad to be strangers to love.
churches look the other way,
they ignore the vulnerable who
weep to sing hymns to tyrants,
while offering last rites to people
entwined by despots who place
them by the hour in graves. the
dictators are deaf to God's word
spoken in many ways and they
fancy torture, lying and profit
from darkness they have the
nerve to call light.

LA BODEGA

spray painted names line the
wall of the bodega offering
credit to the poor and selling
wishes. on the block, the
single mothers roaming
its aisles listen to tropical
beats played in the store,
talk with friends, eat delicious
plantain chips and tell where
it hurts. one young woman
examines a plum for signs
of abuse and tells the little
girl with her, organic fruit is
sold at higher prices in the
white supermarkets never set
up on blocks thought downtown
to be ugly. in the bodega the poor
practice language disobedience
by not saying a damn word in
English.

GOOD-BYE

I learned to tell time in
another world that taught
me living requires letting
things go even when you
want to keep them away
from the river that washes
things out to sea. I studied
wordless goodbyes in the
faces of the elderly who
were in the habit of sitting
by open windows eating
sweet bread and listening
to the promises young lovers
made. I recited all the half
truths the priests poured into
us to explain the darkening
so much like the earth before
it knew human beings. today,
good-bye feels like wandering
into a strange land, God willing
sadness, the Valencia Bakery
without bread and those hollow
tombs where too many friends
and a brother have permanently
gone to rest. I am nonetheless
glad to remember you as a beach,
a rooftop, an old Jewish couple on
the stoop, a single-mother bursting
with prayers, a Polish grade school
teacher, a gentle breeze on a Bronx

morning and all the people who hear
the music that plays for them at the
world's end.

CRYING

leaning into the day I sit
raining tears, signs of past
storms, violins chained to
the church bell towers and
without explanation. I don't
know why I feel a knot in
my throat and this crying that
is a thing coming from beyond?
I pull and drag this wailing like
a thorn bush with moaning roots
and tear after tear rains on the
ground in the name others.

HONEY

I will pull you close to
love with words imagined
by my exclusive alphabet,
hold you near like a wind
flowing through your hair
and whispering secrets in
your ears. no matter where
time places me I know you
like the fragrance of roses
on a wooded path, the way
the sky loves the clouds and
trees the rain. tonight, I will
ask my heart why I love you
more than the Moon, earthly
life and visions of a stunning
paradise. I will put my arms
around you like after a long
absence and laugh while the
crickets share nightly songs
of how you make a mystery
of everything.

THE CHILD

I used a skinny hand to paint
on the school wall the image
of a child with a delicate brown
face, a Saint's halo in bright gold
above his head and a needle stuck
in his arm. his feet had nail holes
on them, his eyes an innocent stare
and to the right of him I painted a
flag with the words beneath it that
said America the beautiful. on the
left corner of the painted image I
could not help writing the words
here you see Joey in the place of
the other kids on the block that too
well know the immaculate descent
into the void of junkie life. the city
is ungrateful, those who toil unable
to see him, and the wind never kissed
lost boys.

THE CREEK

we carried sand bags to the
creek to make a beach on a
bank beside train rails next
to the dark water of the East
River belonging to us. we dove
off a train bridge lifting fists
to signal life capitulated the
darkness and then defiantly
shouted like it was prohibited
in the school yard. the morning
belonged entirely to us, the raft
made from drift wood floating
with Diamond laughing on top
of it and every half-naked dark
body splashing in the dirty water
of the imagined seaside. we were
caressed by the water that listened
to stories, tales of divine causes
learned from Irish priests, and
talk about which skinny Puerto
Rican boy could hold his breath
the longest. we swam better than
Jesus walking on water exploring
with each dive into the creek the
treasure heard in shouts from across
the Atlantic and the tenements on
Simpson Street.

CHANGE

let us depart the home
that cannot remember
times of walking together
to the Cathedral, the stops
of love, the clarity of kids
playing on the streets, the
distance covered by the
old in the wilderness and
the hope junkies find only
between nods. let us look
for the corners visited by
radiant goodness, places
offering water to drink and
where dew still descends on
the sidewalks. let us hope
for magnificent times in the
neighborhood and keep the
memory of broken chains
fresh then take the time to
never wave farewell to yet
another strung out brother,
sister and friend.

LOST

the building is home to
families who lost their
country, the windows
in the apartments offer
no view of mountains,
the furious waves of a
blue sea or sight of the
once upon a time town
squares the abuelas call
plazitas. the newcomers
were welcomed into the
new land by family who
cared and denounced by
strangers who despised
hearing Spanish and seeing
dark skin. if you stumble
someday in the lost country
send a letter to the Lopez
family living in apartment 2C
at 1203 Westchester Avenue
and tell them you happened
to trip on their lost country
one morning in a park, one
day on the beach and over a
suitcase in a hotel about to
be packed for the flight to
the nation of immigrants that
holds them, now.

RAIN

you must remember the
pouring rain one April
when the Catholic kids
dressed up in outfits for
which they saved all year
disappointedly gathered
to lament not being able
to head to the amusement
park that kept them with
smiles. the city a little less
radiant on the stormy day
saw life go on with mothers
off to work, fathers missing,
the super showing up to mop
the tile floor of the neglected
art deco tenement, war in
Central America and Easter
faith in the kids straying like
the rain fall. I wore a brand
new pair of half-snake shoes,
Delancey Street pepper silk
trousers, a new rainbow Alpaca
sweater and a whole bunch of
hair slick for the first time. I
shined lots of old shoes on
Southern Boulevard to buy
that pair of shoes that would put
me on good terms with the rest
of the cool kids on the block
and the things were poorly fitted

so they never did stop pinching.
Man, I never could match the
cool on the block though I was
glad not to take my hurting feet
to the amusement park. we stayed
in the building corridor and I got
the idea to conjure spirits by singing
a little Doo-Wop to match our fancy
Delancey Street threads.

GIRL ON THE STEPS

there is someone sitting on
the stoop tonight handling
stones with signs of age that
were found in the park north
of the East River. my eyes
circle her like the pigeons
flying around the rooftop
with old Italian men guiding
them with red rags tied to the
end of long bamboo poles.
I confess feeling peace and
thinking the world entirely
before me in the shadows on
the stoop, stones about to spit
up syllables, music floating out
of Carmen Julia's ground floor
apartment window and the girl
that walked to school with me
each morning sharing an endless
smile. from that day forward I
asked for no more than to know
what it means to kiss, to love and
close my eyes with her. when I
remember the block , it is that
night on the stoop with heaven
leaning to meet us.

DWELLING

in the tiny apartment on Mapes
Avenue in a building once the
dwelling of Jewish immigrants,
in cramped rooms talking Spanish
with the scent of coffee lingering
in the space, she recalled the roses
shared by grandmothers in her
village who came to give blessings
for the journey she was about to
make to flee suffering caused by
civil war. she agreed to a new life,
working seven days a week for four
days' pay, messaging family back
home in the twilight of lonely hours
when her eyes would not shut for
sleep. sometimes, she sat crying
and strained to hear voices in the
air she imagined floating to her
from across the border to patch
the holes in her twenty-year-old
heart. these memories lived in her
like the dancers in the Catholic school
she once attended and she followed
them in the city with mostly white
faces whose unenlightened blabber
left a knot in her throat.

PROTEST

in the old city like many
others we have a voice,
it is painted on the building
walls, subway cars, cracked
sidewalks, schoolyards, and
in the very world that takes
sides. we have no small voice
since it is stitched together
you see by heaven, protesting
injustice by the installment
plan, confident walls will
crumble and Spanglish will
say it loud on the ground of
the innocent slain. the smell
of paradise will be in written
words, the headstones in the
cemeteries will be kissed and
the nation will lament the fire
of hell earned by its carnival
of hate.

OLD SAN JUAN

the old Spanish colonial
city beneath today's blue
sky skipped to the sound
of drums on streets lined
with rainbow flags made
to dance by a gentle wind
in the name of those who
cherish love more than the
sinister threats uttered by
others. the marchers smiled
with tilted heads gay like
the tropical morning and
tutoring the gawking eyes
of tourists on the mysteries
of love and the thousands of
resurrections celebrated in
the pride parade. I watched
the pageant with my kids in
Old San Juan, recalled the
day in New York when my
uncle introduced me to his
boyfriend and was moved
by the happiness bringing
life to a city where Spanish
colonial terror was replaced
by English names.

WHISTLING

Lord,
let me find the village
with the scent of fresh
flowers, kids busy with
games, elders whispering
happiness before saying
the rosary and someone
I love laughing like the
whistling kettle conjuring
tales.
Lord,
help me forget the barbarity
of war, the violence on the
streets, the police brutality,
the cruelty of power, the well
practiced ignorance of those
backing the executioners of
the poor and the Word made
in their flesh.
Lord,
allow me to look at villages
and the city with you beside
me, to stay the rage in my
spic soul owing to hundreds
of generations pushed into
early graves and despite all
things to dream heaven and
paradise forever.

SIMPLE

love is a collection of
remembered hours with
flowers marking woodland
paths, warmth in a ray of
Autumn sun and the gentle
touch of a sweet slender hand.
love is a fall into open arms,
gravity pushing matter through
clouds and holding each other
by the hand. love is climbing
out from silence, mingling into
union, the heart clattering like a
whip-poor will's song and acts
of life bundled into fullness. love
is older than Moses's cracked slabs,
 more dogged than promises from
the redeeming stable and steadier
than stars lighting up the dark in
the mysterious heavens. love is
above the sky and never ready
to end.

HOLD ME

on the stony road never let
me go, keep me moving with
you toward the dreamy answers
and the places crazy enough for
God to bless. keep me away
from the worldly spaces with a
million sliding games for giving
up and not a single earthly eye
can pause to fix like bread, cup
and wine delivered from beyond
the ticking clocks. remind me of the
names of all the Saints, the places
where the scattered bones of slaves
rest, the people who understand the
languages I speak and the silence left
by those forever missed. hold me
close enough to find love in every
story, the church in testimonies of
freedom and loving everything in
the world heaven does. hold me
until the curtains open on the room
with the ageless chairs inviting us
to rest.

TRAFFICKED

in the beginning, there was a
young girl who flew from an
island after a world war to an
old post-colonial city on the
eastern seaboard of a country
that once ordered tubal ligations
for every child bearing age lady
on her abuelas rock. she escaped
with thirteen years of life, months
of hostility leaving scars on her
back, the toxic men coming out
of sugar cane fields aiming
to steal her innocence and living
with the negligence of an aunt.
the orphaned girl was trafficked
to a sailor who searched for a
helpless child to put in a white
wedding dress, have his three
kids and never notice the child's
horror speaking in silence and
exhibited on her beaten flesh.
after too many years, when the
man was at sea, she enrolled in
Paris Beauty School to acquire
a barber's license to run a shop
where she tilted mostly elderly
Jewish ladies' heads styling hair
to court her freedom with blood
and tears. after being beaten by
the aging seaman, she pierced

the dark with a candle in front of
a bedroom shrine, packed her things,
gathered her kids, and took all her
pain into the night. the aging teen
girl launched a new life finding a
one room apartment with her three
kids, holding her youngest in skinny
scarred arms and declaring this now
is home. she spent weeks trying to
erase the edges of remembered years
in the flaming tower of her prior life
she so daringly jumped. no matter how
she angled experiences in her innocent
years, she clamored about slave wage
work, children to clothe and feed and
loneliness to spare. she reached old age
surprised to see it, heard her first child
died a young man, lost touch for decades
with another, raised a daughter to live in
a world where the sun never came out
after rain and never failed to pray for
the promises of heaven to extend from
her minimum wage labor, section 8
home to the two kids still alive and a
number of grandkids who smile at the
spangled lights on the hillsides they
see—God bless trafficked girls like
my mother!

PUPPY

my puppy loves to tumble
in the grass, stroll the garden
to catch the scent of flowers,
carry large twigs with eyes
saying get a look at me and
age a little more each day with
kids. sadness never fills her
day, perfect love is what she
gives and in her private way
she smiles when rubbed on her
tummy and hugged from room
to room. my puppy knows a
great deal of heaven on earth,
she leads me without a leash,
speaks to me without a word
and knows better than any why
the moon comes out at night
and mockingbirds sing.

LUNCH

the kids spent most of the
public school year hiding
from English, weeping in
Spanish during recess and
looking forward to a lunch
paid by their hard-working
and tax-paying mothers. on
hot summer days they stood
in long lines occasionally
even passing out like drunks
waiting for Jewish and Irish
lunch ladies to open cafeteria
doors to them for a free hot
meal. these women who wore
black scarves tied around their
necks, gobbled samples in the
downtown shops, kept their best
memories in a box and loved to
welcome thin Puerto Rican kids
into the lunchroom to feed them
each until the last hour. the graying
ladies often overheard stories from
the boys and girls that made them
shiver, with fragile hearts they asked
why a wealthy country disfavored
feeding needy kids, and they giggled
when they felt the thousands of kisses
sent in their direction by the hungry
Black and Brown faces smiling before
a big plate of sloppy Joes. these kids

raised by single-mothers with twisted bones who attended school with empty stomachs looked for maps charting a way to greener fields with food to eat and books filled with tales of gigantic dreams.

RALLIES

the rally wars began across midwestern towns, some news shows say there is a difference between a self-interested con man and a fearless Black woman, or a truth telling governor and a phony hillbilly with extreme positions on everything, including the idea that freedom is a misguided thing. the rally wars are underway with one side full of the hate that tightens rope on dark-skinned necks and another offering a way back to the places that beat the darkness and unblock the boundaries of hope, equality and the nearly destroyed doorways of democracy. the rallies are underway with the pompous, pretentious, bullshit artists passing conspiracy theories from beneath their wastes and another declaring unity for a society that will always be dense with multicolored people who dream.

AMERICA

there is a country inside of
them appearing during the
pledge of allegiance in the
local public school, during
the national anthem at the
Yankee game and when they
are told to go back to where
they belong. they invented
Spanglish to sing American,
created break dancing that is
today an Olympic sport, sat
on stoops naming stars, eating
sugar cane, inhaling summer
nights, while the next generation
played beside them. their blood
is red like everyone, though their
hands are dark and scarred by an
imagined white nation. there is a
country inside of them weeping
and when dark clouds settle over
them they picture the American
dream that always speaks in many
tongues.

THE OTHER SIDE

in the summer, we spend hours
talking about things like living on
the other side of the river, seeing
tenements with Satellite dishes on
rooftops for the first time and the
burdens of hard work keeping us
from rising no matter how gentle
the breeze brushes the cheeks of
the blameless children skipping
rope. for several months we have
thought about the river bejeweled
with concertina wire that claimed
the life of a young mother along
with her toddler and disgraceful
official language in a tranquil day
told citizens to look away. on the
other side of the river, many things
take us back to the past when we
were property, lived with shackles,
wept in the silent spaces of night
and could not figure out just how
we fit with God in the places that
grew churches. in the summer, those
of us tossed aside laugh and celebrate
what we shape into life in the name of
a new creation.

THE WORKERS

they have worked hard the
long week, the elder man
who talks of the Viet Nam
war, the lady with a broken
arm, the single-mother with
two boys working on a GED,
the teen living in the building
across the street from the dog
park who quit High School to
work downtown and grow old
collecting tales. they lived the
summer of 1968 when the Beatles
premiered Yellow Submarine, police
clashed with anti-war protestors in
Chicago, Nixon and Agnew were
nominated by the GOP, two Olympic
athletes raised gloved fists, Martin
was murdered in Memphis and riots
held the streets. they lived beyond
the urban fires, found time to laugh
in broken days and believed love
would have the last word.

THE KITE

I came down from the roof
flying paper scraps like a
kite. the sky that morning
saw diamonds sailing in
the wind, box kites flown
above streets and ships
sailing lofty realms like
the pigeons flown from
coups on the roof of the
building still a dwelling to
Italian immigrants who did
not check white in any box
on government forms, hardly
spoke any English and saw
sit-ins and civil rights marches
on black and white televisions
that made their way to them
from white homes. my kite
made from used notebook
paper was like an Angel in
flight drifting on thread with
kids cheering for it to be set
free.

END OF THINGS

the vultures grouped in
the sky circle the valley
over agonizing flesh nearing
a last gasp. in this empire's
war death filling unmarked
graves is not a blessing and
only the poor, the nameless,
the easily forgotten are killed
in the name of a God backing
violence. Silvia who fled the
capital dressed wounds on the
mountainside for young men
and women with mouths not
sewed shut by those who own
the world where mother's buy
flowers for the dead. now, too
many years later, the poor who
suffered, trusted God, blessed
priests and the revolution ask
themselves is love the last word
for a world in need of the divine
gift of life.

THE DEN

there is
an
abandoned
building
on
Fox Street
no pipes
in
the kitchen
and
bathroom
no
glass windows
a hole
in a
door
once for
a lock
cylinder.
linoleum
carpet
ripped
from
wood floors
no beds
for sleep
just a
junkie
behind

a
door
selling
dope
by way
of
the hole
to
kids
from
the lost
street.
no
names
for God
are
ever
spoken
and
children
like
other
opioid
fiends
happen
to be
murdered
nightly
by
dope.

DUSK

love happened on the stoop
at sundown when the music
started to pour out of a first
floor window. it came even
to the heart of youth entirely
unexpectedly like light from
a freshly lit candle, a silvery
full moon above a dreamy
head or like the whispering
shore of the Caribbean sea.
love happened that night with
the scent of Autumn, congas
sending messages and stars
brightening at the sound of your
blameless laughter. perhaps, that
is why with closed eyes, I can see
you moving toward me saying, "I
love you."

THE CONVENTION

tonight, candles brilliantly
lead us through the dark,
democracy sings from the
land of Lincoln for all the
world to hear and chilled
eyes on the other side and
mouths spilling distasteful
words cannot hold back the
coming days possessed by
hope. tonight, in the land
of the man pierced by the
nails of a divided nation
and familiar to darker flesh,
sadness is swept away by
a fresh new wind and light
is slowly filtering into us
pushing away the old man
playing Craps in our heads
and everyone it appears is
finding love for the place
becoming like Langston
wrote the dream it used to
be, a place of love and foe
to tyrants, kings and people
of greed too small to dream
America, remade.

VOTE

they are weeks away from
voting day talking out loud
in the kitchen about the need
for better days, the bedroom
mattresses undressed, the kids
hungry in the long school day,
the bad news talked about on
the corners, blaring in Spanish
on the radio and from the smelly
mouth of the landlord who comes
around to collect the rent they
can hardly pay. the price of food
high every day of the year for
these people paid petty wages
to break their backs and kneel
at home in front of their altar of
Saints asking to hit the numeritos.
everybody wants a vote around
their neighborhood like the owner
of the funeral parlor, the baton swinging
cops, teachers collecting checks,
lawyers hustling the undocumented
and politicians marching left or right
who promise the poor a better life.
their children pledge allegiance to a flag
that recalls these new Americans in the
name of condescension and old women
in church who say they are citizens
declare this time one vote counts for
people who cannot be lynched, beaten
or sold.

THE WAYS

like the central city library full of
books on topics even unimagined
there are so many ways to think of
God, the first and absolute reality,
the unnamed, and the One known
by Emi who has not read everything
and has a clear view from the pew
that welcomes her and the window
in her tenement where she often sits
to watch the streets below and sing
church songs. like many religions
on this circling earth, Emi feels the
sweetest love from heaven roving
deep within her, floating quietly in
the waters of her Spanglish mind
and lighting up the darkness refusing
to understand that all roads travel the
same creation made beautiful by the
gods that hold us close and the One
she calls by name. this woman who
often prays with a minor tremor in her
wrinkled voice says she just craves
more light in the world that thinks
of God in many ways.

SILENCE

after sitting beneath a
cashew tree enjoying the
sun's gold rays finding a
way past her shading
leaves it occurred to me
the old sapling loved
the rain that fed it, the
moon lighting its dark
nights, the family eating
her gifts and everyone who
praised her for sitting year
after year in the middle of
the yard with God. there
was nothing that day to be
done save enjoy the birds
that paused on the tree's
branches to sing, distant
barking from lost dogs
traveling by the creek
and kids kicking a ball
in their very own World
Cup. before too long the
poor family from a house
on the hillside came to sit
in the shade with and silence
became for us over the next
hour a sacred tongue.

LAMP POST

on West Farms Road, the
lamp post rusting for years
glowed bright in the darkness
for kids. it worked lunar nights
holding memories belonging to
people strolling and it glowed
in early morning light chasing
away murky plots without ever
mumbling a word. sometimes,
when day ended the kids got
out their favorite music boxes
and borrowed a little electricity
to play sounds and move skinny
bodies in ways the white media
called breakdancing though the
style witnessed by the lamp post
is part of hip hop writ large born
in the days of urban decay. the
old lamp post always managed
to give light like a lover offering
flowers with a kiss.

THE BOOKS

this was the first day of
school in P.S. 66, pencils
sharpened, empty writing
paper, thoughts shifting by
the seconds, white teachers
proudly trying out Spanish
and kids full of American
made dreams. this was the
Autumn season, imposingly
chilly, imagined hiding the
heavenly mansion in plain
sight of day. this was the
first visit to a book mobile
in front of school, the way
it smelled like dusty books
whispering pick me.

THE SUBWAY

I love the subway
before rush hour
with near empty cars
refined by stillness.
the way few riders
enter a wagon at each
station smiling before
reaching their place for
a weary day of work.
I love the way light is
close to us in dark tunnels
like love in novels written
by authors who describe
a closeness never saying
good-bye. I love to see
lovers holding hands with
light in their eyes shining
wherever the cars darken
like ripples made by rocks
tossed into the Central Park
lake. I love the way morning
rises like a curtain opening on
a stage giving everyone a place
and without fussing telling us
enough to be here and exist for
the next few minutes until the
stop.

POETRY PATH

on the lower west side of
the city around Battery Park
not far from where the poor
shiver and tourists come to
look across the bay at Lady
Liberty you will find a place
called Poets House. the park
established more than a hundred
years ago, has monuments on
its grounds to soldiers, immigrants,
explorers and inventors, and now
you will find fragments of poems
along a lengthy path with things
to say of the connection between
people, nature, and all manner of
urban things. here you will find
the words of poets reaching across
cultures, speaking in many tongues,
talking of bus stop love, the clouds
in passing and the sweetest lyricism
to haunt readers dreams. you must
come walk down this poetry lane to
see benches spinning, iron rails on
which sweethearts lean, and rejoice
in the spot where not a single word
will be left out of the history books
guiding the inquisitive to the harbor
of ancient sea air and precious
worth.

THE DOOR

we have been looking for
the open door on the Wall
for days, one that says come
in, hablamos español, stop
wandering around in the dark,
there are no cops to put you
in cuffs, and you can sit with
skinny white men and women
to drink cafe without wasting
away in petty wage lettuce fields.
we have searched for the spot
where mail easily crosses the
border with letters for the poor
living in the North, for people
West of New York and North
of Texas who are awake in well
set dreams that learned to speak
an English tongue. we will keep
looking for the door, feel elated
sitting beneath cloudless nights
and pray no one in either side of
the border counted among those
who belong forgets us.

THE RIDE

when you have no words left
to pray hop unto the subway
for an underground trip across
the city. remember not to look
back at the church, bother about
the names of stations or feel the
slightest fear of the dark. recall
old stories shared by abuelas of
Spanish speaking lands, dreams
whispered by people in the church
basement queued for confession,
and young single mothers with hurt
at the altar waiting for a dramatic
divine entrance. remember to see
riders half-asleep in the car who
speak mixed English, more than a
few who embody one of the 800
languages that immigrated to this
city considered no longer a far away
place. mingle with the rush hour
crowd by strolling between the cars,
make your way downtown then
come back on the Spanish Harlem
track. finally, returning to the beginning
where you are not a stranger, exit
the metal wagon that carried you
passed many stations complete with
shadows to light.

TOSSING

you have tossed and
twisted in bed with bad
dreams, wet the pillow
with tears, shouted of
memories left behind
and in the dark I called
your name with no more
than an embrace. sweet
darling a nightmare did
stumble into your sleep
this gloomy night. I
gently woke you and
watched it retreat while
angelic light came to rest
with you.

THE STOREFRONT

after the shouting in the
storefront church, people
exit the space searching
for the miraculous signs
imagined in their spirit
driven service. the stray
dogs come out of alleys
and they are sent away
by old women lost in
theological imaginings
of a sort. the junkies on
the corner who have not
visited the church remain
beyond the understanding
of the pious who still hear
tambourines and barked
prayers in heads cloaked
from messy lost streets.
on Southern Boulevard
businesses selling cheap
goods are open, an old
man invites people to play
three-card Monty and the
lush promises of heaven
are flown by pigeons to
Hunts Point Market just
to sing hymns.

HAIR

on hot summer days some
kids in other neighborhoods
let their hair down when they
go out to play. still, many of
us on the block favored perfectly
entangled hair worn as a beautiful
bush. mother warned me not to
listen to those who said they wanted
to fix my big Puerto Rican natural,
police my mixed race and change
the precious kinks God gave me.
people who were enslaved for
centuries, denied a place in
God's creation, brutally treated
and frequently lynched by white
hate live in every curl on the top
of my head that snags the teeth
of combs sold in the white stores
doing business on occupied land.

FRENCH RESTAURANT

I walked passed the French
restaurant in Old San Juan
with no particular destination
when the owner of the eatery
invited me to work that night
scrubbing pots in the kitchen
to remove the food clinging
to them. at fourteen, I was
glad to have the offer of a
job that came like answered
prayer I admired the French
cook who spoke a little Spanish
who asked me with a Parisian
smile to work until 2:00 AM.
from my sink, I saw people in
the dining room, including a
couple in one corner of the
room, smoke threading above
theme from cigarettes held by
manicured fingers. at the end
of my round, the owner of the
restaurant wanted me back the
following day though I declined
and he refused to pay me for the
night of work. I did not argue with
the French man's flawed logic and
I believed Pascal's abyss would be
permanently carried on back. perhaps,
that experience explains my aversion
for French restaurants and the blades

waiting to be displayed by the tongues
of arrogant proprietors.

SLUM

to those of you who have
never visited a tenement
with repaired glass in the
stairwell windows, children
yelling games in the halls
with dreams unraveling like
Oscar winning movies, mothers
coming out of apartments with
futures in their eyes, dogs in
alleys emptying cans for scraps,
junkies rushing to rooftops to
break open bags for a fix and
priests not visiting. to those among
you who have never said a Spanish
name, have given up on finding hope
prospering, never imagined words that
bubble up from wounded hearts and
look away from the tangled world of
zealous witnesses to better days in
American slums. I say to you walk
among us like the gods of old and
the man from Nazareth who rises
with us.

MEDITATION

in front of the bedroom
altar Saints standing in
candlelight not making
a sound a few words of
prayer are enough, after
silence followed by breath
in the world not talked of
tonight.

STREET WALKER

in the Aguacero restaurant
seated in a corner table she
caught a glimpse of herself
in a mirror only to quickly
look away unable to keep
from seeing images of the
men who picked her up on
the street and passed their
paying lips over her skin.
her body cringed thinking
about nights fingers danced
on her brown thighs before
handing over a few bucks she
used to get a fix. sometimes,
alone on Simpson Street Rosa
felt she lived in a borrowed
body, other times she wondered
what it was like to love or how
many more nights she would
spend crying on her back and
staring at a ceiling waiting for
answered prayers or life to be
entirely her own. we were in
the fifth grade together and I
have watched her wither like
a flower for more years than
priests have served in the local
church and more days than I
can remember sitting on the
stoop with her imagining the
promised land.

THE BORDER

borders cannot keep wind
from blowing, birds from
flight, names shouted from
drifting long distances or
love from settling wherever
it wishes. the artificial line
cannot keep migrants from
gathering with the things they
carry inside nor will it keep
legs from crossing. the wall
will not impede us from hanging
rosaries on it and in the spaces
of silences nothing can prevent
us from writing names on steel
to tearfully tell former foreigners
who live on occupied land to listen
while we speak of the hollow places
left by those paid to have us slowly
turn to dust. the border will never
stop us from finding light beneath
stars nor answers on God's earth
made without limits.

SIGNS MATTER

we cannot propose a toast for his
dark impulses, the invitation to
racial fear, the incoherent sentences
about never letting the oppressed go
free, the delusional visions offering
nothing good for America, and his
reckless clutch on anger and perfectly
articulated stupidity. we will not forget
his posing for pictures in front of a church,
signing God bless you Bibles to resell,
golden high-top sneakers hawked, nor
peddling of digital trading cards, a mugshot
suit and rips of cloth from what he wore
when a piece of his ear was allegedly shot
clean off. we will not lift a single glass for
this sniveling old man imagining the earth
is flat, laughing at the global poor forced
to beg for bread and full of purple mountain
bullshit. we will not allow the abominable
con man to ransack homes of decency, enjoy
his false tales about dark-skinned immigrants
eating cats and dogs, freed from mental asylums,
poisoning white blood, invading the nation and
eager to commit unthinkable crimes. we will
never agree with the delusional thinking of a
criminal man standing at the edge darkness,
shaking little fists, charming idiots, forgetting
what he last said and claiming he alone makes
America great. now, we lift cups today in the
name of the truth and justice that heaven itself

will allow to crash on the unenviable crook's inflated head.

ANNIVERSARY

when the civil war ended in
that little country with family
and friends shouting about the
joys of heaven come to earth,
a beautiful thing happened to
us in the time and space God
made. love came for us when
villages no longer trembled and
birds in song returned to them.
after many years, my hands reach
eagerly to hold you and store your
touch deeply in me. in the present
you make, I often lay awake recalling
all the times of blessing that began
the first day together and I imagine
will continue until time ends with
a magnificent new dawn.

THE PITCH

I walked to the end of the
pier to toss a bottle filled
with votive prayers from
single mothers who lived
in the same building with
Cuca. they trusted me to
carry their wishes to the
sea believing a cola bottle
would float to the very place
the earth begins and find its
way to the hand of God. the
jetty was a familiar place and
I promised to fling the bottle
far from the shallow coastline
and away from the ships in
the bay aiming for a Brooklyn
port. in the moments before
the pitch, I offered few words
to the healer above sometimes
found among things in our old
tenements.

INVISIBLE

the mystery that has kept me
many years, in childhood in a
common church, in family from
a common spring, on the block
with a spirit I could not see, on
rooftops with a vast silence never
filled is yet here. this mystery once
followed me on the wide avenue
when I chased flower petals down
the sidewalk, it was with me the
night I spotted on the canopy of
the Freemen Street train station
a nest with birds diving into flight
and I was sure they were friends
sent back to life. this mystery cried
out from civil war fields, refugee
camps, clandestine jails, box cars
with migrant riders, Rikers Island
jail cells, troubled public schools,
the tender poor, and the innocent
with grief suspiciously overlooked
by light. the mystery despite the
wounds I have seen and those I
know is a thing allowing us all to
weep, laugh, and live.

PUERTO RICO

after the hate festival at
Madison Square Garden
in the city that has been
home to Puerto Ricans
for more than a hundred
years, nobody present woke
to bigotry on the rally stage
landing like a cold front on
the long-aggrieved. we never
were the things imagined by
the foul-mouthed asshole paid
to get laughs. we are the sorrow
of colonialism, the beautiful people
of an enchanted island unbroken
by American lunacy, the sofrito
children of a crucified God with
names that move silence, factory
workers, service providers, doctors,
lawyers, teachers, cops, scientists,
athletes, pilots, astronauts, composers,
musicians, artists, writers and Supreme
court judge. we are living on occupied
land, tired of being stooped over star
spangled things, patching up sliced skin
and suffocating in a nation with many
churches nodding approvingly for White
supremacy.

CHAOS

chaos is the new daily fix
from the right that spreads
like an illness and feels like
a big knife stabbing us in a
darkness where God even
manages to get lost. for the
unforgiving chaos that wakes
with us each morning the best
minds no longer find words to
explain the strange house made
for us and the relentless cruelty
giving rise to unspeakable new
developments. chaos is the face
of elected leadership that lashes
the back of equality and defiles
the beautiful word, democracy.
chaos is the ranting madness of
the phony strong man never to
be a future king and it haunts
us more than dogs in an alley
welcoming thieves.

RAIDS

silence in a society driven
by hate that has been for
several hundreds of years
etched in dark skin has a
home in church. the work
place raids taking place in
cities have not rounded up
criminals, damage working
class lives, flatten citizen kids
and indiscriminately grab the
dark skinned. there is a word
that makes us shiver by day
and weep at night, these days
its shouted on the playground,
in schools, and a few churches
whispering its terror from pew
to pew for families to flee once
again, la migra! silence is now
the American Christian way
and it dreams of bigger Walls
and smaller tables for the devil
to feast with those holding fast
to what is low, merciless and
faithless.

AGING

each year provides another
wrinkle that drops in without
announcement delivering news
that often does not suit us. the
latest truths begin to occupy us,
memory weakens and our hearts
are impressively delighted to feel
another passing season. sometimes,
we spend the hours keeping track of
the new passengers carried by an aging
body no less a refuge for the innocent
child inside of it. we have been given
many years to dream in worlds with
much in them to love and for places
where not a wrinkle will revoke hope
rolling around like pebbles in the sand
in places dear to us. perhaps, now you
dear friend will share an anthology of
stories with us until the last leaf on the
church yard tree falls.

.